Date Due

MAR 15 '91	Ck		
MAR 19 '91			
MAR 25 '91			
APR 30 '91			
MAY 16 1991			
MAY 30 1991			
JUN 7 '91			
NOV 28 1991			
JAN 22 1992			
MAY 15 '92			
MAR 1 2 1996			
MAR 1 5 1996			
JAN 2 5 1999			

Discard

JUNIOR PET CARE

TURTLES

ZUZA VRBOVA

Photography Susan C. Miller
Illustration Robert McAulay, Hugh Nicholas
Reading and Child Psychology Consultant
Dr. David Lewis

Additional photography by William B. Allen, Jr.; Dr.
Herbert R. Axelrod; Tom Caravaglia; Isabelle Francais;
Dr. P.C.H. Pritchard; Harald Schultz; A. van den Nieu-
wenhuizen.

With special thanks to Kim and Len Simmons, Linton Zoological Gardens,
Pat and Tony Lear, Jenny Toft at Pet Bowl, Andrew Menzies, Menor
Photographic Services.

Library of Congress #89-52059

Distributed in the UNITED STATES by T.F.H. Publications, Inc., One T.F.H. Plaza,
Neptune City, NJ 07753; in CANADA to the Pet Trade by H & L Pet Supplies Inc.,
27 Kingston Crescent, Kitchener, Ontario N2B 2T6; Rolf C. Hagen Ltd., 3225 Sar-
telon Street, Montreal 382 Quebec; in CANADA to the Book Trade by Macmillan of
Canada (A Division of Canada Publishing Corporation), 164 Commander Boulevard,
Agincourt, Ontario M1S 3C7; in ENGLAND by T.F.H. Publications, The Spinney,
Parklands, Portsmouth PO7 6AR; in AUSTRALIA AND THE SOUTH PACIFIC by
T.F.H. (Australia) Pty. Ltd., Box 149, Brookvale 2100 N.S.W., Australia; in NEW
ZEALAND by Ross Haines & Son, Ltd., 82 D Elizabeth Knox Place, Panmure, Auck-
land, New Zealand; in the PHILIPPINES by Bio-Research, 5 Lippay Street, San Lor-
enzo Village, Makati Rizal; in SOUTH AFRICA by Multipet Pty. Ltd., Box 235 New
Germany, South Africa 3620. Published by T.F.H. Publications, Inc. Manufactured in
the United States of America by T.F.H. Publications, Inc.

CONTENTS

1 The Nature of a Turtle   *page* **6**

2 Choosing a Land Turtle   *page* **14**

3 A Home For Your Land Turtle   *page* **20**

4 Feeding your Land Turtle   *page* **26**

5 Care for Your Turtle   *page* **30**

6 Choosing a Water Turtle   *page* **34**

7 A Home for Your
      Water Turtle   *page* **38**

8 Feeding Your Water Turtle   *page* **44**

Some Common Ailments   *page* **46**

Glossary   *page* **48**

NOTE TO PARENTS

Owning a pet can be an important part of growing up,
helping a child learn about the pleasure of giving and
caring. These are new experiences for a child. *Turtles*
has been specially written for children of age seven and
upwards. It introduces a child to a loving
and affectionate animal.

Being written in a lively and informative way, bearing the
young age of the reader in mind, *Turtles* will help a
child to understand and relate to the needs of others
from an early age. Owning a turtle and caring for it
properly will promote qualities of care and understanding
that are important to us all.

THE NATURE OF A TURTLE

Turtles are lovable pets and fun to look after. They are quiet and independent animals. Just like us, every turtle has a personality of its own.

The turtle shell

The first thing you notice about turtles is their shell. This is certainly an appealing part of a turtle's make-up. After all, wouldn't we all like to have a real protective shell that we could hide in when we were frightened or in trouble?

The shell encloses the whole of the body. A turtle cannot live without it. Only the turtle's head, tail and legs stick out of the shell. The top part of the shell, called the **carapace** (kara-pase) is joined along the sides of the body to the lower half of the shell, called the **plastron**. The bony plates of the shell are covered with hard, horny material that is made of material similar to our fingernails.

Turtles are reptiles

Turtles are part of a large group of animals called reptiles. Some other animals in this group are lizards, snakes and crocodiles. They share some basic features. All reptiles have scaly skin. You will notice this as

Looking after a turtle is fun.

soon as you look at the legs, head and tail of a turtle. But turtles are the only reptiles that have a shell.

The female turtle does not give birth to a baby turtle, but instead she lays eggs. In each egg, a new baby turtle develops and grows until it is ready to hatch out of the egg and explore the world.

Temperature control

Turtles, like all other reptiles, cannot keep themselves warm the way we can. The inside of our bodies is controlled so that it is always at the same temperature—even on a very cold day or a very hot day.

Turtles, though, cannot do this, so they become cold inside if the weather is cold and warm when the sun is shining. This is why turtles are always more active on a hot day. They like to sunbathe, to warm to up their bodies. On a cold day, you will notice that your turtle moves more slowly and is sleepy.

Temperature is very important for a turtle, and one of the first things to learn about turtle-keeping is to be aware of the temperature of the air. You must always ensure that your turtle is warm.

The long sleep

Many wild turtles find a cozy and safe place to sleep for the winter until the warmth of the spring awakens

them. This is called **hibernation.** Although it might be possible for you to provide conditions under which your turtle can hibernate, it is safer to keep it active by giving it good conditions to live under all year long.

Turtles and dinosaurs

Part of the fascination of turtles is that their lifestyle and appearance are very different from ours. Tur-

tles look as though they could almost have come from another planet. The first turtles flourished at a time when the Earth was a very different kind of planet. Turtles used to roam the lands and swim in the sea, just as they do now, 200 million years ago when they lived alongside the dinosaurs.

Dinosaurs have been extinct for some 60 million years, but turtles have survived. They have lived

This Aldabra turtle is 15 years old. He is still a youngster, as he might well live to be 200 years old.

through all the changes that affected the Earth millions of years ago—the same ones that may have caused the extinction of the dinosaurs. Many people find turtles intriguing simply because they have existed almost unchanged for such a long time.

Turtles are remarkable in other ways. They live for a very long time. They can often live longer than we do. This is why buying a turtle is a long-term commitment. Some turtles live for more than a hundred years. If you look after your turtle well, you could even pass it on to your grandchildren to look after.

Land and water turtles

Some turtles live on land and some turtles live in water. Some turtles found on land are called **tortoises.** Most tortoises come from the hot, dry lands of the world and have a domed and deeply patterned shell. Water turtles live in marshes, ponds and rivers. Here they swim and catch snails, frogs, worms and fish. They have a flatter shell so they can swim more easily, and unlike land turtles they have webbed feet. Some turtles also live in the sea.

If you decide to buy a turtle, the first decision you must make is whether to buy a land or a water turtle.

Water turtles like sunbathing on rocks.

CHOOSING A LAND TURTLE

If you would like to keep a turtle as a pet, the best thing to do is to go to a pet store. There you will see some of the different kinds of turtles that there are to choose from.

You will be able to identify the turtle by the markings on its shell. It is a good idea to find out the kind of turtle you are buying so that you will know how to look after it properly and guess what size it may grow up to be. Larger turtles, over five inches (12 cm), can be easier to keep than smaller ones.

When choosing your turtle, bear in

mind that the ones you see in the pet store will grow quite quickly in the first few years. When they are grown-up turtles, they will need plenty of space to move around in. That is why you should make sure that the terrarium in which you keep your turtle is large enough to house it as an adult as well as while it is very young.

Selecting a healthy turtle

At the pet store, look at several turtles carefully before you decide which one you want. Hopefully, you will

Baby turtles grow quickly during their first few years. Take care not to drop your turtle and to handle it carefully.

then choose
a strong, healthy
turtle to take home.
Your young turtle should have bright, sparkly open eyes. It may be a little bit shy and withdraw quickly into its shell when you come up to look at it closely. It will soon grow to like you without being frightened.

Look at the shell carefully to make sure that it is not damaged. Then,

ask a grown-up to show you how to pick the turtle up. It is useful to take note of how heavy and big the turtle is in comparison with its companions.

A healthy turtle will often struggle when you first handle it. Its legs will seem strong and move back and forth. Look at the legs for any cuts that might become infected. Check the claws, too, in case they need to be cut later.

The eyes should be clear. Check

that the turtle does not have a runny nose. A grown-up who is used to handling turtles could open the mouth for you to look inside. The turtle should have a bright, fleshy pink tongue.

Ticks live on turtles and other animals. They usually are not dangerous, but look out for any hiding on the turtle's body, often in the places where legs join the body. They are about the same size as your finger nail. A grown-up can help you remove a tick by rubbing petroleum jelly over it. It will then drop off after a day or so.

Handling your turtle safely

It is important for you and your family to know that turtles can have an illness called **salmonellosis** (sal-mon-nel-o-sis) in their bodies. It does not harm the turtle, but you can catch it and it will make you ill, as if you had bad food poisoning. To avoid this, wash your hands every time after you handle your turtle or its enclosure. As you probably know, it is always best to wash before eating and after handling any animal, and certainly before you touch food.

Baby turtles like this Mississippi map turtle are safe to pick up, but you must wash your hands after doing so.

A HOME FOR YOUR
LAND TURTLE

Although land turtles often move very slowly, they are good at climbing and scurrying away and escaping forever. They like to wander freely in your back yard. But if you let them wander they might dig up your parents' favorite flower beds and eat the flowers.

Also, neither tortoises nor other land turtles can live outside for more than just a short period of the year in most areas of the United States. In general, it is best to keep your turtle inside the house. Doing so lets you have greater control over the temperature and humidity and other factors that greatly affect your turtle's health. It also keeps your turtle safe from stray neighborhood cats and dogs. But if you live in an area that lets you keep your turtle safely outside the house, the following sections will give you some good tips to follow.

A turtle enclosure

To allow your turtle to enjoy its freedom and at the same time not damage your garden, it is best to make a special area for its home. This is called a

run. Making a run will also prevent your turtle from escaping. The run should be as large as possible.

As turtles are remarkably good climbers, the height of the run needs to be twice the length of your turtle. Also, it is best to use wood to make the sides of the run, as turtles will often try to climb over wire netting and they may hurt themselves.

Inside the enclosure, your turtle needs to have a little house for shelter during bad weather and to sleep in at night—similar to your house and garden. Many turtles put themselves to bed in their cozy den at the same time every evening.

Turtles are creatures of habit and if you put them in their new house several times, they will soon enjoy being there in a safe, sheltered spot.

Your turtle's bed

You will need to provide some bedding material inside the turtle's house to keep it snug and warm at night. Torn-up strips of newspaper make a

soft, warm bed for the turtle to burrow into. Straw is a little too sharp and prickly to use as bedding material. It can damage a turtle's eyes. You may use hay as a bedding material, but make sure it is completely dry or it can make your turtle ill.

It is bedtime for this turtle.

Where to make the run

Turtles need to be kept in a warm dry place. They also need to be able to find shade from the sun on very hot days. Bearing this in mind, decide which patch of your lawn to put the run on. Inside its enclosure, your

Water is very important for your turtle. Inside the run you must have a shallow bowl of fresh water. Most turtles prefer the bowl to be big enough to bathe in as well as drink out of.

turtle should be able to look for interesting plants to eat, just as it would do naturally in the wild.

Water

Water is very important for your turtle. Inside the run you must have a shallow bowl of fresh water. Most turtles will like it if the bowl is big enough for bathing as well as drinking. Dig a hole for the water bowl so your turtle will not knock the container over. Remember to change the water every day.

Two different types of turtles that live on land.
Above, a desert tortoise from the southwestern
United States; below, two red-footed tortoises from
South America.

FEEDING
YOUR LAND TURTLE

Land turtles tend to be mostly vegetarians. They mainly eat green food like garden plants, vegetables and fruit. They do not eat meat very much or very often—if they do, it will only be in small amounts.

Turtles have individual tastes, just as people do. When you first bring your pet turtle home, it will be interesting to find out what foods your turtle likes to eat.

To make sure that your turtle is fed all the necessary vitamins and minerals, you should offer it a variety of green food. You can also buy a supplement to sprinkle over its food. Turtles do like to forage for their

Land turtles like plantain leaves, clover and chick-weed. A sure favorite for some land turtles is a plate of rose petals and dandelion leaves (above).

own food in the garden, as they do in the wild, but a turtle that is left to wander about the garden to find its own food is very likely to be underfed.

Besides the weeds and flowers your turtle will find in the garden, it needs a selection of vegetables like beans and peas. Other delicacies that you can feed your turtle are cut-up pieces of tomato, cucumber, plums, strawberries and apples.

A little meat should be fed to some turtles. **Box turtles** must be offered meat every day—they eat more meat than other land turtles. They like canned cat or dog food. Box turtles also catch worms and snails in the garden, so be careful that they are not poisoned by chemicals. Always offer your turtle fresh food. Wash greens and fruit before giving them to your turtle—just as if you were eating them yourself. You can leave the water on the food after you have washed.

Feeding times

Turtles are browsing animals. They nibble at one plant and then move on to the next. Therefore, it is a good idea for you to give them small amounts of food two or three times a day, rather than one big meal.

They like to have a routine, so it is best to feed them at the same time in the same place each day.

Poisonous foods

Rhubarb leaves are poisonous to turtles, and buttercups tend to give them tummy upsets too. Do not allow your turtle to wander on grass that has recently been treated with weedkiller, which is very poisonous.

CARE FOR YOUR TURTLE

Although turtles are quiet and independent animals, they do need attention every day and should not be left to fend for themselves. For example, your turtle may have an accident and fall over onto the top part of its shell. It may not be able to roll over on its own, and you will have to turn it the right way up again.

Food supplements

Calcium—which helps to make our teeth, nails and bones hard—is important for a turtle's shell and bones too. Since the calcium levels in plants are low, use a mixed mineral and vitamin powder made just for turtles to keep the shell in good condition. Ask for this at your pet store.

Weighing your turtle

When you first buy your turtle, one of the most important parts of caring for it is to take note of how much it is eating. Some turtles do not eat properly when they are settling into their new home.

To ensure that your turtle is putting on enough weight, weigh your turtle regularly. The best way to do

SHELL CARE

A turtle's shell is made of living, growing material. Drilling into or cutting into a turtle's shell will hurt the turtle.

At first, the most important part of caring for your turtle is to take note of how much it is eating. Some turtles do not eat properly when they are settling into their new home.

this is by putting your turtle in a strong carrier bag before placing it on the scales. A new-born baby is weighed every week for the same reasons—it is very difficult to tell whether it is taking enough food. If your turtle is not putting on weight or is losing weight, take it to a veterinarian because it may not be well.

Write down the weight of your turtle each time you weigh it so that you have a record of how well it is growing.

CHOOSING A
WATER TURTLE

There are several different kinds of water turtles that you can buy in pet stores. In the wild, water turtles live mostly in water. As pets they are kept in large containers full of water, called **tanks**, with a dry area on the side.

Red-eared turtles have a distinctive red stripe behind each eye. You can easily recognize them by looking for the stripe. Red-ears come from the lower Mississippi Valley, mostly from Louisiana. As youngsters they have a shell length of only an inch or so, but when they are grown up they can be up to 8 inches (20 cm) long. They might be a little nervous when you first bring them

The red-ear turtle is a water turtle that comes from the southern part of the United States. It is perhaps the most common pet turtle in the world.

home, but they will soon calm down and become tame.

35

Selecting a healthy water turtle

When you go to the pet store to choose your young turtle, look at all of them in the tank carefully. Take note of the ones that look most lively and scurry readily into the water. One of the more active ones will be best for you to have as a pet, as it is most likely to be fit and healthy. You can keep two together, but if you do this make sure you have a large tank.

A water turtle that just sits on a

rock with its eyes closed may not be very well. Besides choosing a lively, alert youngster, look at the shell of your water turtle to make sure that it is healthy-looking and not damaged.

You will need to buy a heater for your tank to keep the water warm enough for your turtle. If you buy a thermometer you will be able to check the water temperature. A temperature of 75 to 85°F (24 to 30°C) will be good for your turtle.

This American snapping turtle is a water turtle that is very hardy. Unfortunately, it also can be dangerous.

A
HOME FOR YOUR
WATER TURTLE

Water turtles have a different lifestyle and different feeding habits to land turtles and so looking after them is different too.

You may be able to keep your water turtle in a large tub, or a pond from a pet store sunk into the garden during the summer. You can then bring them indoors and keep them in a tank of heated water in the winter. An old bath tub sunk into the ground can make a comfortable, pond-like home for your water turtles.

Alternatively, you can keep your turtle in a tank indoors all year 'round.

Hibernation

In the wild, the water turtle would burrow into the mud in the bottom of a stream or pond. If you keep your water turtle in an outdoor pond, it could be left to hibernate by burrowing into the mud at the bottom. The mud in your pond or tub must be at least 12 inches (30cm) deep for the turtle to hibernate in.

Soft-shell turtles are water turtles that almost never leave the water. They are not friendly.

A tank for your turtle

Before you bring your new turtle home you will need to make a comfortable tank to put your water turtle in. The ideal place to buy a tank for your water turtle is from a pet store. Young water turtles grow quickly and so it is best to buy as large a tank as possible. Water turtles like to have plenty of space to swim about in. To make the tank similar to the turtle's home in the wild, first line the tank with one or two inches of gravel. This is available from most pet stores. You can even buy it in different colors—bright blue or red—which will make your turtle's tank an even more attractive feature of a room.

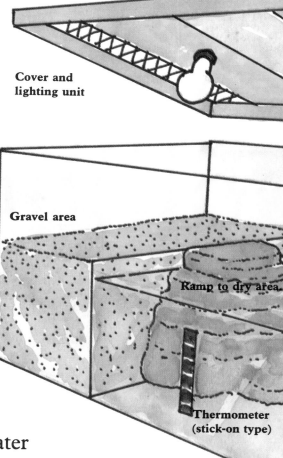

Cover and lighting unit

Gravel area

Ramp to dry area

Thermometer (stick-on type)

You will also need to buy a heater for your tank to keep the water warm enough for your turtle. If you buy a thermometer you will be able to check whether the water is warm enough for your turtle.

Light for your turtle

Water turtles need light to keep their shells healthy. When setting up the tank, a grown-up will need to attach a light above the tank. It should be on for only eight hours a day but will help to keep the air temperature warm.

A sunbathing area

Your water turtles will need a place to lounge in when they are out of the water. To make this, use some stones for a rocky area, similar to a river bank, but make sure the turtles can climb out of the water easily.

When your tank is ready, you can fill it with ordinary tap water. It should be at least six inches (15 cm) deep to give your turtles enough room to swim about in.

Submersible heater

Cleaning the tank

You can buy very efficient filters from a pet store to keep the tank clean. If there is no filter in the tank, the water will have to be changed at least twice a week.

Sun and exercise

We need some natural sunlight to provide us with vitamin D, and water turtles are the same. If you keep your water turtle in an indoor tank, it is a good idea to have a spare small tank outside to allow your turtles to sun-bathe on hot sunny days. This will also help to stimulate their appetites. The tank should be uncovered, but make sure that the water is no hotter

than 85°F (28°C).

In the wild, most water turtles spend some time walking on land. They need this kind of exercise when they are kept as pets. To make sure you have a healthy turtle, it is a good idea to allow your turtle to take a walk outside the tank on a fine day. Naturally, you must watch your turtle carefully to make sure it does not escape or come to any harm.

This water turtle blends in with the rock onto which it has climbed to bask in the sun.

FEEDING YOUR WATER TURTLE

Water turtles eat a wide range of food. They like meat and fish, and to make sure they have a balanced diet you should also offer some vegetables.

The ideal way of feeding water turtles is to use a complete turtle food which you can buy from a pet store. This will contain all the nutrients and vitamins your turtle needs.

Some young turtles are reluctant to eat at first, but they are usually tempted by live food such as the small thin red worms available in most pet stores as food for tropical fish. They are usually sold as "tubifex" (too-bee-fex) worms. If you find any snails or worms to give your turtle, try to check that they have not been covered with insecticides or any other dangerous chemicals.

Also, when you give your turtle vegetables, make sure they are cut up into small pieces. Remember, a good varied diet is an important part of keeping your turtle healthy.

This American box turtle is one of the most popular land turtles. It is an easy turtle to feed.

SOME COMMON AILMENTS

At some time during its life, your land or water turtle may become ill or injured and may need veterinary treatment. If your turtle stays in one place for a long time during warm weather or refuses food on a warm day in the summer, it might be ill and you should ask a grown-up to help you take it to a veterinarian. Pet shops sell good remedies for common turtle ailments.

Soft shell

This is when the shell becomes soft and deformed. It sometimes happens to water turtles if they are kept in an indoor tank because glass that the tank is made of does not allow the sun's ultraviolet rays through. These are the beneficial rays that make vitamin D in the turtle's body, and in your body too. The best cure is to take your turtle out on sunny days, allow it to sunbathe as much as possible, and feed it with a balanced diet of complete food available from pet stores. A lack of calcium can also be the cause of soft shells. Scraping cuttlefish bone onto the food might help your turtle recover.

Eye trouble

Sometimes you may notice that your water turtle cannot open its eyes properly; or, they might look cloudy, without their usual bright sparkle. This could be due to either a lack of vitamin A or too much chlorine from tap water in the tank. Pet stores sell products which make the tap water safe. If your turtle does not recover, take it to a veterinarian without delay. An injection of vitamin A may cure your turtle.

Land turtles sometimes have eye trouble after hibernation. This may also be due to a vitamin A deficiency.

46

Colds and pneumonia

If your water turtle has a runny nose and cannot stay underwater for long, it may have a cold or even pneumonia. Some turtles may even make a whistling sound when trying to breathe if they are suffering from a bad cold. Pneumonia may be caused by a draft near the tank. Heating the water and using a cover may help, but if the symptoms do not clear, take your turtle to see a veterinarian.

Land turtles can get colds too. The symptoms are similar to when we get colds—a runny nose and watery eyes. The turtle may get better if you take it indoors and let it enjoy the warmth of your home— just like when you stay in bed for a while. Make sure the temperature indoors is 75°F (24°C) and keep your turtle out of any drafts. You can use a lamp to heat its quarters.

Not eating

Sometimes turtles lose their appetite. With water turtles this could be because the temperature of the tank is too low. The tank temperature should be raised to 80–85°F (26–29°C). Land turtles too may be too cold to eat and may need to be force-fed by hand for a while if raising the temperature doesn't help. You will need to ask a veterinarian to show you how to open your turtle's mouth and feed it properly and safely.

First aid

If your turtle's limbs are cut by accident, simply apply some antiseptic cream. You might need to put on a bandage, especially if there are lots of flies around. Treat it just as if you have a scraped knee from a fall.

GLOSSARY

Box turtle A kind of land turtle that has a hinge on the lower shell or plastron.

Calcium A food supplement necessary for turtles to grow hard shells and strong bones.

Carapace The top part of a turtle's shell.

Plastron The bottom part of the turtle's shell, covering the undersection of its body.

Salmonellosis An illness in turtles that is generally harmless to them but can be harmful if passed to humans. If this is the case, the person will be sick, as if he had food poisoning.

Tortoises Some dry land turtles are called tortoises; they are distinguished by their domed and deeply patterned shell.